Singularities

Other books
by Susan Howe

Singularities

Susan Howe

Wesleyan University Press
Middletown, Connecticut

Published by
WESLEYAN UNIVERSITY PRESS
Middletown, CT 06459
www.wesleyan.edu/wespress

Originally produced in 1990 by Wesleyan/
University Press of New England, Hanover, NH 03755

Printed in the United States of America

Some of these poems first appeared in *Conjunctions, Sulfur, Acts, Ironwood, Hambone, Io, Temblor, Potes and Poets,* and *Zuk. Articulation of Sound Forms in Time* was published as a chapbook by Awede, 1987.

The epigraph by H. D. is reprinted from *H. D. Collected Poems, 1912–1944,* © 1982 by the Estate of Hilda Doolittle, by permission of New Directions Publishing Corporation.

Library of Congress Cataloging-in-Publication Data

Howe, Susan.
    Singularities / Susan Howe. — 1st ed.
    p.   cm. — (Wesleyan poetry)
    ISBN 0-8195-2192-2 — ISBN 0-8195-1194-3 (pbk.)
    I. Title. II. Series.
PS3558.0893S5   1990
811'.54 — dc20   89-16445

She was looking for the fragments of the dead Osiris,
dead and scattered asunder, dead, torn apart, and thrown
in fragments over the wide world.

D. H. Lawrence

under her drift of veils,
and she carried a book.

H. D.

Contents

Articulation
of
Sound Forms
in Time

*from seaweed said nor repossess rest
scape esaid*

I
The Falls Fight

Land! Land! Hath been the idol of many in New England!
                                            Increase Mather

Just after King Philip's War so-called by the English and shortly before King William's War or Governor Dudley's War called the War of the Spanish Succession by Europeans, Deerfield was the northernmost colonial settlement in the Connecticut River Valley. In May 1676 several large bands of Indians had camped in the vicinity. The settlers felt threatened by this gathering of tribes. They appealed to Boston for soldiers, and a militia was sent out to drive away Squakeags, Pokomtucks, Mahicans, Nipmunks, and others. The standing forces were led by Captain Turner of Boston. Captain Holyoke brought a contingent from Springfield; Ensign Lyman, a group from Northampton. Sergeants Kellog and Dickinson led the militia from Hadley. Benjamin Wait and Experience Hinsdale were pilots.

"The Reverend Hope Atherton, minister of the gospel, at Hatfield, a gentleman of publick spirit, accompanied the army."

The small force of 160 men marched from Hatfield on May 17, shortly before nightfall. They passed the river at Cheapside where they were heard by an Indian sentinel who aroused his people. Indians searched the normal fording place but the colonial militia had missed it by accident. Finding no footprints they assumed the sentry had been deceived by the noise of moose passing along the river. The colonial troops continued on their way until they happened on an unguarded Nipmunk, Squakeag, Pokomtuck, or Mahican camp. This they immediately attacked by firing into the wigwams. Wakened from sleep the frightened inhabitants thought they were being raided by Mohawks. The chronicler writes: "They soon discovered their mistake but being in no position to make an immediate defense were slain on the spot, some in their surprise ran directly to the river, and were drowned; others betook themselves to their bark canoes, and having in their confusion forgot their paddles, were hurried down the falls and dashed against the rocks. In this action the enemy by their own confession, lost 300, women and children included."

What the historian doesn't say is that most of the dead were women and children.

Only one white man was killed at what came to be called *The Falls Fight*. Indian survivors soon rallied neighboring bands and when they realized that the English force was only a small one, they pursued and harassed the victorious retreating army. Now thirty-seven soldiers were killed and several more wounded. The soldiers were retreating because they had run out of ammunition. The retreat soon became a rout. About twenty members of the militia stood their ground and fired at the pursuing Native Americans who were crossing the river. After a hard skirmish they rejoined the body of the now surrounded army, and together they fought their way ten miles back to safety. Except for Hope Atherton and seven or eight others who were somehow separated from their fellows. These Christian soldiers soon found themselves lost. After hiding in the woods for several days some of them came to the Indians and offered to surrender on the condition that their lives would be spared. But the Squakeags, Nipmunks, Pokomtucks, or Mahicans, instead of giving them quarter, covered each man with dry thatch. Then they set the thatch on fire and ordered each soldier to run. When one covering of thatch was burnt off, another was added, and so these colonists continued running, until, Indians later told the historian: "Death delivered them from their hands."

Prophesie is Historie antedated;
and History is Postdated Prophesie.
John Cotton

In our culture Hope is a name we give women. Signifying desire, trust, promise, does her name prophetically engender pacification of the feminine?

Pre-revolution Americans viewed America as the land of Hope.

"The Reverend Hope Atherton, minister of the gospel, at Hatfield, a gentleman of publick spirit, accompanied the army."

Hope's baptism of fire. No one believed the Minister's letter. He became a stranger to his community and died soon after the traumatic exposure that has earned him poor mention in a seldom opened book.

Hope's literal attributes. Effaced background dissolves remotest foreground. Putative author, premodern condition, presently present what future clamors for release?

Hope's epicene name draws its predetermined poem in.

I assume Hope Atherton's excursion for an emblem foreshadowing a Poet's abolished limitations in our demythologized fantasy of Manifest Destiny.

EXTRACT *from a* LETTER *(dated June 8, 1781)*
of Stephen Williams to President Styles:

"In looking over my papers I found a copy of a paper left by
the Rev. Hope Atherton, the first minister of Hatfield, who
was ordained May 10th, 1670. This Mr. Atherton went out
with the forces (commanded by Capt. Turner, captain of the
garrison soldiers, and Capt. Holyoke of the county militia)
against the Indians at the falls above Deerfield, in May, 1676.
In the fight, upon their retreat, Mr. Atherton was unhorsed
and separated from the company, wandered in the woods some
days and then got into Hadley, which is on the east side of the
Connecticut River. But the fight was on the west side. Mr.
Atherton gave account that he had offered to surrender him-
self to the enemy, but they would not receive him. Many peo-
ple were not willing to give credit to this account, suggesting
he was beside himself. This occasioned him to publish to his
congregation and leave in writing the account I enclose to
you. I had the paper from which this is copied, from Jonathan
Wells, Esq., who was in the fight and lived afterward at Deer-
field and was immediately acquainted with the *Indians* after
the war. *He* did himself inform *me* that the *Indians* told *him*
that after the fall fight, a little man with a black coat and
without any hat, came toward them, but they were afraid and
ran from him, thinking it was the Englishman's God, etc., etc."

2
Hope Atherton's Wanderings

Prest try to set after grandmother
revived by and laid down left ly
little distant each other and fro
Saw digression hobbling driftwood
forage two rotted beans & etc.
Redy to faint slaughter story so
Gone and signal through deep water
Mr. Atherton's story Hope Atherton

———————

Clog nutmeg abt noon
scraping cano muzzell
foot path sand and so
gravel rubbish vandal
horse flesh ryal tabl
sand enemys flood sun
Danielle Warnare Servt
Turner Falls Fight us
Next wearer April One

———————

Soe young mayde in March or April laught
who was lapd M as big as any kerchief
as like tow and beg grew bone and bullet
Stopt when asleep so Steven boy companion
Or errant Socoquis if you love your lives
War closed after Clay Gully hobbling boy
laid no whining trace no footstep clue
"Deep water" he *must* have crossed over

———————

Who was lapt R & soe grew bone & bullet
as like tow and as another scittuation
Stopt when Worshp Steven boy companion
Abt noon and abt sun come Country Farm
Follow me save me thither this winter
Capt. Turner little horn of powder
Medfield Clay Gully hobbling boy
Sixteen trace no wanton footstep rest
Soe struck fire set the woods on fire

———————

Two blew bird eggs plat
Habitants before dark
Little way went mistook awake
abt again Clay Gully
espied bounds to leop over
Selah cithera Opynne be
5 rails high houselot Cow
Kinsmen I pray you hasten
Furious Nipnet Ninep Ninap
little Pansett fence wth ditch
Clear stumps grubbing ploughing
Clearing the land

———

Antagonists lay level direction
Logic hail um bushell forty-seven
These letters copy for shoeing
was alarum by seaven bold some
Lady Ambushment signed three My
excuse haste Nipmunk to my loues
Dress for fast Stedyness and Sway
Shining at the site of Falls Jump
Habitants inning the corn & Jumps

———

Rash catastrophe deaf evening
Bonds loosd catcht sedge environ
Extinct ordr set tableaux
hay and insolent army
Shape of so many comfortless
And deep so deep as my narrative
our homely manner and Myself
Said "matah" and "chirah"
Pease of all sorts and best
courtesy in every place
Whereat laughing they went away

---

rest chondriacal lunacy

velc cello viable toil

quench conch uncannunc

drumm amonoosuck ythian

———

scow aback din

flicker skaeg ne

barge quagg peat

~~sieve catacomb~~

stint chisel sect

———

Otherworld light into fable
Best plays are secret plays

———————

Mylord have maize meadow

have Capes Mylord to dim

barley Sion beaver Totem

W'ld bivouac by vineyard

Eagle aureole elses thend

———————

Impulsion of a myth of beginning
The figure of a far-off Wanderer

Grail face of bronze or brass
Grass and weeds cover the face

Colonnades of rigorous Americanism
Portents of lonely destructivism

Knowledge narrowly fixed knowledge
Whose bounds in theories slay

Talismanic stepping-stone children
brawl over pebble and shallow

Marching and counter marching
Danger of roaming the woods at random

Men whet their scythes go out to mow
Nets tackle weir birchbark

Mowing salt marshes and sedge meadows

———

Body perception thought of perceiving (half-thought

chaotic architect repudiate line Q confine lie link realm
circle a euclidean curtail theme theme toll function coda
severity whey crayon so distant grain scalp gnat carol
omen Cur cornice zed primitive shad sac stone fur bray
tub epoch too fum alter rude recess emblem sixty key

Epithets young in a box told as you fly

Posit gaze level diminish lamp and asleep(selv)cannot see

is notion most open apparition past Halo view border redden

possess remote so abstract life are lost spatio-temporal hum

Maoris empirical Kantian a little lesson concatenation up

tree fifty shower see step shot Immanence force to Mohegan

blue glare(essence)cow bed leg extinct draw scribe   upside
even blue(A)ash-tree fleece comfort(B)draw scribe   sideup

Posit gaze level diminish lamp and asleep(selv)cannot see

MoheganToForceImmanenceShotStepSeeShowerFiftyTree

UpConcatenationLessonLittleAKantianEmpiricalMaoris

HumTemporal-spatioLostAreLifeAbstractSoRemotePossess

ReddenBorderViewHaloPastApparitionOpenMostNotion *is*

blue glare(essence)cow bed leg extinct draw scribe   sideup
even blue(A)ash-tree fleece comfort(B)draw scribe   upside

Loving Friends and Kindred:—
When I look back
So short in charity and good works
We are a small remnant
of signal escapes wonderful in themselves
We march from our camp a little
and come home
Lost the beaten track and so
River section dark all this time
We must not worry
how few we are and fall from each other
More than language can express
Hope for the artist in America & etc
This is my birthday
These are the old home trees

———

3
Taking The Forest

Corruptible first figure
Bright armies wolves warriors steers

scorned warning captive compulsion

Love leads to edge
Progress of self into illusion

Same and not the same
Cherubim intone their own litany

Universal separation
—Distant coherent rational system

Vault lines divergence
Atom keystone

Parmenides prohibition
End of passageway perceive surrounding

Consciousness grasps its subject
Stumbling phenomenology

infinite miscalculation of history

Great men thicker than their stories
sitting and standing

to mark suns rising and setting
Ridges of sand rising on one another

Mathematics of continua

fathomless infinitesimal fraction
sabbatical safety beyond seven

Empty arms cloud counterfeit

antecedent terror stretched to a whisper

———

Certain autumnal story

absent humanity
Mothers from their windows look

Forth now
Sunbeam

oakleaf wreathe possible symbol

splitting nature's shadow
splitting the world

hammer at nature to temper Terrible

Range loom and lacing Clear
companion

shuttle face lost   Prelude
Straw portion

seed to be called Sarah's laughter

Dodge tinder huge hush
dodge thoroughfare outside since

Heard trace tidings

Complexity kissing sense into empty

Thread gone
Tongue collect song

Logical determination of position

Scuttle and striving

Being into never ending sequence of

Becoming
Coming home through past ages

visible light on the legionnaires' banner
with welcoming welcoming

and undersweeping

————

Double penetrable foreign sequel
By face to know helm

Prey to destroy in dark theme
Emblem of fictitious narrative

Step and system

Collision and impulsion
Asides and reminders to myself

Lives to be seen pressing and alien

Fix fleeting communication

Carried away before a pursuer
Demonstration in a string of definitions

To walk a little
Night's kingdom lamentation dimming

Snatched idea
Recollection fallen away from ruin

Slide into elect unalterable

slipping from known to utmost bound

Paper plague odd ends reap

Faint legend is day
Mahomet touched a flower with the tips

of his fingers
Face of the voice of speech

Flaming heart on the extended hand
Sky red and lowering

Mountains pitched over to westward

———

Invisible festival
halves drawn into a circle

feigned necessity vanished from memory

Hymn to the light
hymn and psalm to the light

Eight points of a compass

mosaic pattern eastward dispelled

Summoners slip into ritual
Planctus of Rachel

Shadowy figures of the Magi
elongated figures trooping in stone

Parallel column
Geographical assertion

Straw mother heaved higher and higher
Self ceded to sphere

Pull world around streets
Prosper our journey

Class structure belonging to shelter

migratory odd scrap trilogy

Laughter hallows the house in summer
Thin home hover in theme

———

Far away at a periphery

Celt heaven
Lugboat of children thousand in superstition

streak is the sky
sliver of shimmering

disputation in dominion beyond sovereign

Puck's face of earth
Sign and laughingstock Puck

Fable into fretted parable flew off
An old theme frolicking

Walk on the ramparts

headlong dwindled to span

Predecessor and definition
incoherent inaccessible muddled inaudible

Speech was a cry for action

erroneous proof
erroneous choice

axe-edge wording of each ramping lion
whirlwind handwritten

Commonwealths kindle and climb

Tender scudding visible
My body goes out alone as I came

nameless numberless no plan

Chaos cry carrion empirical proof proving
Summary succession of spectators twisted

away

———

We turn suddenly

Lords of the Lay

Letters sent out in crystalline purity

Muddled and ravelled

Sigh by see

Smoke faces separate

Lore and the like

Sucked into sleeping

—Hegelian becoming

—Hugolian memory

Patriarchal prophesy at heels of hope

Futurity—

———

Shouting an offering

Messengers falter

Obedient children elder and ever

Lawless center

Scaffold places to sweep

unfocused future

Migratory path to massacre

Sharpshooters in history's apple-dark

———

Bound Cupid sea washed

Omen of stumbling
Great unknown captaincy

centuries roam audible silence
whissing days roam own key

Second time somewhere

seclusion in symbol sovereign

Memory mutinies contours cling

Mother my name
pin-eyed children

sundial lair from mortal fear

hooed Peru

Prisoned stone guardian
guerdon of resurrection

fictitious deeps

Cries open to the words inside them
Cries hurled through the Woods

———

Threadbare evergreen season
Mother and maiden

Singing into the draft

Keen woes centuries slacken
woe long wars endurance bear

In forest splinter companion

essential simplicity of Thought
wedged back playmate of Remote

Hares call on Pan
To rhyme with reason revels run

———

Untraceable wandering
the meaning of knowing

Poetical sea site state
abstract alien point

root casket tangled scrawl

Mistletoe arrow
ascetic hero-shadow

Shelter secret in heart
were wound drawn out

Rhyme of Heaven open

Collision with human protection

———

Left home to seek Lost

Pitchfork origin

tribunal of eternal revolution
tribunal of rigorous revaluation

Captive crowned tyrant deposed
Ego as captive thought

Conscience in ears too late

Father the law
Stamped hero-partner

pledge of creditor to debtor

Destiny of calamitous silence
Mouth condemning me to absence

—Uneasy antic alibi

dimmed dimmest world
final fertile mantle of family

Leap from scratch to ward off

———

Home in a human knowing

Stretched out at the thresh
of beginning

Sphere of sound

Body of articulation chattering

an Assassin
shabby halo-helmet

hideout haystack hunter chamois

History of seedling and seduction
Kinship of infinite separation

Sight of thought

Crooked erratic perception
shoal ruin abyssal veil veiling

Braggart expert
discourse on dice

Face to visible sense gathers moss

———

Freedom's dominion of possible

Ear to parable
lilies spin glory

Adamant glides architrave front

Path to blest vanishing
kindled oracle vanishing

Stripped of metaphysical proof
Stoop to gather chaff

Face to fringe of itself
forseen form from far off

Homeward hollow zodiac core

omen cold path to goal

End of the world as trial or possible
trail

———

The Now that is Night
Time comprehended in Thought

Sullen chill uncertain
Solitude and chill uncertain

Glacier cloud drifting

nimbus of extinction
mimic tracery mimic swaddling

week of dull day under hell-sky

All things double on one another
On to pure purpose

Spinoza the lens grinder
Lenses and language

total systemic circular knowledge
System impossible in time

truant freedom of dream

Wishes fly off
Tender consecration of garden

frost ends the rose
november affirmation in negation

Shear against easternmost

eternal Ideal sequence
Out among haphazard children

sunny investigations of Permanence

———————

Philology heaped in thin

hearing
Cult code mediation

(Cult cairn)
Symbol allotted to ocean

Talker
and intellectual attacker

edging and dodging

Outer shallow mute

Mackerel sky
wind-ripples

Legend of the King's hill

name of wildflowers
roost in neighboring

Scuffle eminence peacock keeper

Sign of sound
sibilant wind

Scanned chronicles clasp edges

rag veracity
ring of our bodies

Names are bridges to coast

permanence

Naked figure moving in color all flower

———

Occult ferocity of origin

each winged ambition
sand track wind scatter

Inarticulate true meaning

lives beyond thought
linked from beginning

Pilings of thought under spoken

Physiognomy of Liberty

far friend forever Nestling
Forfeit mortality

Cycles snare mastery
headlong centuries cycles ensnare

Face answers to face
limit and quiet Limit

Field of vision and field of future

Shadowy Icarian figuration

Vision closes over vision
Standpoint melts into open

wanton meteor ensign streaming

———

Girl with forest shoulder
Girl stuttering out mask or trick

aria out of hearing

Sound through cult annunciation
sound through initiation Occult

Enunciate barbarous jargon
fluent language of fanaticism

Green tree of severance
Green tree girdled against splitting

Transmutation of murdered Totem

Foresters move before error
forgotten forgiven escaping conclusion

Oak and old hovel grow gossamer

————

Shoal kinsmen trespass Golden
Smoke splendor trespass

Symmetry carried from country
frail counterfeit well met

Lost among equivocations
Emancipator at empyrean center

Anarchy into named theory
Entangled obedience

muffled discourse from distance
mummy thread undertow slough

Eve of origin Embla the eve
soft origin vat and covert

Green hour avert grey future
Summer summon out-of-bound shelter

———

Hook intelligence quick dactyl

Bats glance through a wood
bond between mad and made

anonymous communities bond and free

Perception crumbles under character
Present past of immanent future

Recollection moves across meaning
Men shut their doors against setting

Flocks roost before dark
Coveys nestle and settle

Meditation of a world's vast Memory

Predominance pitched across history
Collision or collusion with history

Summary of fleeting summary
Pseudonym cast across empty

Peak proud heart

Majestic caparisoned cloud cumuli
East sweeps hewn flank

Scion on a ledge of Constitution
Wedged sequences of system

Causeway of faint famed city
Human ferocity

dim mirror Naught formula

archaic hallucinatory laughter

Kneel to intellect in our work
Chaos cast cold intellect back

———

Hemmed trammels of illusion
rooted to shatter random

Firstborn of Front-sea
milestone by name farewell

Milestones bewitched millstones
Sleep passage from Europe

Otherworld light into fable

Negative face of blank force

Winds naked as March
bend and blend to each other

Fledgling humming on pathless

Old Double and old beginning
Vain Covergesture

———

Latin ends and French begins

Golden page third voyage
Caravels bending to windward

Crows fly low and straggling
Civilizations stray into custom

Struts structure luminous region
Purpose or want of purpose

Part of each kingdom of Possession

Only conceived can be seen
Original inventors off Stray

Alone in deserts of Parchment
Theoreticians of the Modern

—emending annotating inventing
World as rigorously related System

Pagan worlds moving toward destruction

———

Visible surface of Discourse

Runes or allusion to runes
Tasks and turning flock

Evening red enough for chivalry

Algorithms bravadoes jetsam
All Wisdom's plethora pattern

paper anacoluthon and naked chalk

Luggage of the prairie
Wagons pegged to earth

Tyrannical avatars of consciousness
emblazoned in tent-stitch

Five senses of syntax

Dear Unconscious scatter syntax
Scythe mower surrender hereafter

Dear Cold cast violet coronal

World weary flesh by Flesh bygone
Bridegroom

———

Last line of blue hills

Lost fact dim outline

Little figure of mother

Moss pasture and wild trefoil
meadow-hay and timothy

She is and the way She was

Outline was a point chosen
Outskirts of ordinary

Weather in history and heaven

Skiff feather glide house

Face seen in a landscape once

———

To kin I call in the Iron-Woods
Turn I to dark Fells last alway

Theirs was an archheathen theme
Soon seen stumbled in lag Clock

Still we call bitterly bitterly
Stern norse terse ethical pathos

Archaic presentiment of rupture
Voicing desire no more from here

Far flung North Atlantic littorals

Lif sails off longing for life
Baldr soars on Alfather's path

Rubble couple on pedestal
Rubble couple Rhythm and Pedestal

Room of dim portraits here there
Wade waist deep maidsworn men

Crumbled masonry windswept hickory

———————

Thorow

During the winter and spring of 1987 I had a writer-in-residency grant to teach a poetry workshop once a week at the Lake George Arts Project, in the town of Lake George, New York. I rented a cabin off the road to Bolton Landing, at the edge of the lake. The town, or what is left of a town, is a travesty. Scores of two-star motels have been arbitrarily scrambled between gas stations and gift shops selling Indian trinkets, china jugs shaped like breasts with nipples for spouts, American flags in all shapes and sizes, and pornographic bumper-stickers. There are two Laundromats, the inevitable McDonald's, a Howard Johnson, assorted discount leather outlets, video arcades, a miniature golf course, two run-down amusement parks, a fake fort where a real one once stood, a Dairy-Mart, a Donut-land, and a four-star Ramada Inn built over an ancient Indian burial ground. Everything graft, everything grafted. And what is left when spirits have fled from holy places? In winter the Simulacrum is closed for the season.

I went there alone, and until I became friends with some of my students, I didn't know anyone. After I learned to keep out of town, and after the first panic of dislocation had subsided, I moved into the weather's fluctuation. Let myself drift in the rise and fall of light and snow, re-reading re-tracing once-upon

Narrative in Non-Narrative

I thought I stood on the shores of a history of the world where forms of wildness brought up by memory become desire and multiply.

Lake George was a blade of ice to write across not knowing what She.

Interior assembling of forces underneath earth's eye. Yes, she, the Strange, excluded from formalism. I heard poems inhabited by voices.

In the seventeenth century European adventurer-traders burst through the forest to discover this particular long clear body of fresh water. They brought our story to it. Pathfinding believers in God and grammar spelled the lake into *place*. They have renamed it several times since. In paternal colonial systems a positivist efficiency appropriates primal indeterminacy.

In March, 1987, looking for what is looking, I went down to unknown regions of indifferentiation. The Adirondacks *occupied* me.

Gilles Deleuze and Felix Guattari have written in an essay called "May, 1914. One of Several Wolves?": "The proper name *(nom propre)* does not designate an individual: it is on the contrary when the individual opens up to the multiplicities pervading him or her, at the outcome of the most severe operation of depersonalization, that he or she acquires his or her true proper name. The proper name is the instantaneous apprehension of a multiplicity. The proper name is the subject of a pure infinitive comprehended as such in a field of intensity."

Thoreau once wrote to a friend: "Have you ever observed how many of the Indian names of rivers, lakes, &c., end in *et*? Assawampset, Acushnet, Pascaamanset, &c., &c. I am informed by a person who appeared to have some knowledge of Indian words that *et* signifies water—the Taunton river was called Nemasket for several miles from its outlet from the Middleborough Ponds—then Tetiquet or Tetiquid. Now I come to my object—did not your Musketaquid have the final syllable *quet*?

Sir Humfrey Gilbert wrote in *A New Passage To Cataia*: "To proove that the Indians aforenamed came not by the Northeast, and that there is no thorow passage navigable that way."

Work penetrated by the edge of author, traverses multiplicities, light letters exploding apprehension suppose when individual hearing

Every name driven will be as another rivet in the machine of a universe flux

Henry David Thoreau to Daniel Ricketson.

—am glad to see that you have studied out the history of the ponds, got the Indian names straightened—which means made more crooked—&c., &c.

Daniel Ricketson to Henry David Thoreau.

My dear old Northman, sitting by the sea,
Whose azure tint is seen, reflected in thy e'e,
Leave your sharks and your dolphins, and eke the sporting
   whale,
And for a little while on milder scenes regale:
My heart is beating strongly to see your face once more,
So leave the land of *Thor*, and *row* along our shore!

Mrs. Daniel Chester French, *Memories Of A Sculptor's Wife.*

Thoreau I was never fortunate enough to see. . . . I loved to hear the farmers talk about him. One of them used to say:

    'Henry D. Thoreau—Henry D. Thoreau,' jerking out the words with withering contempt. 'His name ain't no Henry D. Thoreau than my name is Henry D. Thoreau. And everybody knows it, and he knows it. His name's *Da-a*-vid Henry and it ain't been nothing but *Da-a*-vid Henry. And he knows that!'

I

Go on the Scout they say
They will go near Swegachey

I have snow shoes and Indian shoes

Idea of my present
not my silence

Surprise is not so much
Hurried and tossed about
that I have not had time

From the Fort but the snow
falling very deep
remained a fortnight
Two to view the Fort & get a scalp
domain of transcendental subjectivity
Etymology the this

present in the past now
So many thread

———————

Fence blown down in a winter storm

darkened by outstripped possession
Field stretching out of the world

this book is as old as the people

There are traces of blood in a fairy tale

————

The track of Desire
Must see and not see
Must not see nothing
Burrow and so burrow
Measuring mastering

When ice breaks up
at the farthest north
of Adirondack peaks
So empty and so empty
Go back for your body
Hindge

———

Dear Seem dear cast out
Sun shall go down and set

Distant monarchs of Europe
European grid on the Forest

so many gether togather
were invisible alway Love

———

at Fort Stanwix the Charrokey
paice

only from that Alarm
all those Guards

Constant parties of guards
up & down

Agreseror

Bearer law my fathers

Revealing traces
Regulating traces

The true Zeno
the immutable morality

Irruptives

thorow out all
the Five Nations

To cut our wete

of the Jentelmen

Fort the same
Nuteral

Revealing traces
Regulating traces

To Lake Superior to view
that time the Shannas & Dallaways
Home and I hope passage
Begun about the middle next
to Kittaning

Eating nothing but hominey
Scribbling the ineffable
See only the tracks of rabbit
A mouse-nest of grass

_____

The German Flatts
Their women old men & children
Numerous than I imagined
Singing their War song
I am
Part of their encroachment

Speed & Bleave me &
a Good Globe to hang in a hall
with light

_____

To be sent in slays
if we are not careful
To a slightly place
no shelter

Let us gether and bury
limbs and leves
Is a great Loast
Cant say for us now
Stillest the storm world
Thought

———

The snow
is still hear

Wood and feld
all covered with ise

seem world anew
Only step

as surveyor of the Wood
only Step

———

2

Walked on Mount Vision

New life after the Fall
So many true things

which are not truth itself
We are too finite

Barefooted and bareheaded
extended in space

sure of reaching support

Knowledge and foresight
Noah's landing at Ararat

Mind itself or life

quicker than thought

slipping back to primordial
We go through the word Forest

Trance of an encampment
not a foot of land cleared

The literature of savagism
under a spell of savagism

Nature isolates the Adirondacks

In the machinery of injustice
my whole being is Vision

———

The Source of Snow
the nearness of Poetry

The Captain of Indians
the cause of Liberty

Mortal particulars
whose shatter we are

A sort of border life
A single group of trees

Sun on our back

Unappropriated land
all the works and redoubts

Young pine in a stand of oak
young oak in a stand of pine

Expectation of Epiphany

Not to look off from it
but to look at it

Original of the Otherside
understory of anotherword

———

Thaw has washed away snow
covering the old ice

the Lake a dull crust

Force made desire wander
Jumping from one subject

to another
Besieged and besieged

in a chain of Cause
The eternal First Cause

I stretch out my arms
to the author

Oh the bare ground

My thick coat and my tent
and the black of clouds

Squadrons of clouds

No end of their numbers

Armageddon at Fort William Henry
Sunset at Independence Point

Author the real author
acting the part of a scout

———————

The origin of property
that leads here Depth

Indian names lead here

Bars of a social system
Starting for Lost Pond

psychology of the lost
First precarious Eden

a scandal of materialism

My ancestors tore off
the first leaves

picked out the best stars
Cries accompany laughter

Winter of the great Snow
Life surrounded by snows

The usual loggers camp
the usual bark shelter

Fir floor and log benches

Pines seem giant phenomena

Child of the Adirondacks
taking notes like a spy

————

Most mysterious river

On the confined brink

Poor storm
all hallows

and palings around cabin

Spring-suggesting light

Bustle of embarkation
Guides bewildered

Hunt and not the capture

Underthought draws home
Archaism

Here is dammed water

First trails were blazed
lines

Little known place names

tossed away as little grave
pivot bravura

———————

Long walk on Erebus

The hell latch Poetry

Ragged rock beside hemlock
Mist in deep gulfs

Maps give us some idea
Apprehension as representation

Stood on Shelving Rock

The cold Friday
as cold as that was

Flood of light on water
Day went out in storms

Well structure could fall
Preys troop free

I have imagined a center

Wilder than this region
The figment of a book

Scarce broken letters
Cold leaden sky

Laurentian system of Canada

Tuesday the instant May

———

Elegiac western Imagination

Mysterious confined enigma
a possible field of work

The expanse of unconcealment
so different from all maps

Spiritual typography of elegy

Nature in us as a Nature
the actual one the ideal Self

tent tree sere leaf spectre
Unconscious demarkations range

I pick my compass to pieces

Dark here in the driftings
in the spaces of drifting

Complicity battling redemption

———————

Cannot be
every
where I
entreat
snapt

Re s o lu t i o n

picked up arrowhead

hieroglyph

Parted with the Otterware

at the three Rivers, & are

Gone to have a Treaty

battereau   with the French at Oswego

At this end of the carry   islet   & singing their war song

neck

sheen   The French Hatchet

drisk

Their Plenipo   squall   Messages

disc   coin   splint   cedar

chip   grease   cusk

lily root

a very deep Rabbit

swamp   of which will not per[mit] of   wavelet

fitted to the paper, the Margins   shrub

mud

Encampt   Fires by night   Frames should be exactly   waterbug

canoes   wood

c o v er y   la v o

Cove

places to walk out to

Tranquillity of a garrison

Escalade

Traverse canon night siege Constant firing

Traverse canon night siege Constant firing

Gabion
Parapet

Gabion
Parapet

Traverse canon night siege Constant firing
Escalade

Tranquillity of a garrison

Places to walk out to
Cove

canoes

waterbug   The Frames should be exactly   wood
Fires by night   Encamp t

mud   fitted to the paper, the Margins

shrub   of which will not per[mit] of

wavelet   a very deep Rabbit   swamp

cusk   grease   chip   coin   lily root

cedar
splint   disc
Their plentipo
sheen

drisk   Messages

The French Hatchet
neck
At this end of the carry
& singing their war song
islet

batteau   The War Belt   hieroglyph   Picked up arrowhead

Messengers say

over the lakes

Of the far nations

57

You are of me & I of you, I cannot tell

Where you leave off and I begin

      selving

      forfending
            Immeadeat Settlem
      but wandering
            Shenks Ferry people
      unhoused
            at or naer Mohaxt
      elect
            Sacandaga vläie
      vision
            Battoes are return
      thereafter
            They say
      resurgent
            "Where is the path"
      laughter

      ankledeep

      answerable   *last*

PASSACAGLIA   Strict counterpoint *reassemble*
  Moon wading through cloud   *Union*

           Stress   *mighty*
    distant day helter No nd
                wa *lenght*
Awake! top hill demon daunt defiant   Premis
               brested
              a
              on
              ce
              If
              first

anthen   uplispth   enend

    adamap   blue wov   thefthe

folled   floted   keen

                        Themis

thou sculling me
Thicfth

I haue determened to scater thē therowout the worlde, ād to make awaye the remēbraunce of them from amonge men.

William Tyndale's Pentateuch,
"Deuteronomye," XXXII. 26

Scattering As Behavior Toward Risk

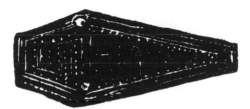

"on a [p<suddenly . . . on a>was shot thro with a dyed→<dyed→a soft]"*
(became the vision) (the rea) after Though   [though]That
Fa

But what is envy [but what is envy]
Is envy the bonfire inkling?

Shackles [(shackles)   ] as we were told the . . . [precincts]

*Billy Budd: The Genetic Text

A Vengeance must be
a story
Trial and suffering
of Mercy
Any narrative question
away in the annals
the old army
Enlightened rationalism

———————

dreadful at Hell
bears go in dens
No track by night
No coming out
in the otherday
on wild thoughtpath
Face of adamant
steel of the face
          Breast

———————

Own political literature

Stoic iconic Collective
Soliloquy and the aside

Suppose finite this is
relict struggle embrace

Violent order of a world

Iconoclastic folio subgenre

a life lived by shifts
evil fortunes of another

Halfway through *Wanderings*
walks the lean Instaurator

Birth of contemporary thought
Counter thought thought out

———————

Loaded into a perfect commonwealth or some idea.

In common.

Bisket
Risk
Herring
More imagined it. The best ordered commonwealth
VIZEADMIRAL Salomon
Ore Watchwords
That Open
Would have no money no private property no markets.
the sayd
Utopian communism comes in pieces while the Narrative wanders.
aboord
Shrowds
Values in a discourse. Potentiality of sound to directly signal
To hull in the night
wavering Meaning
wavering Cape Rase overpast
any bruit
Saxoharmony sparrow or muttering
brawling that lamentation
The overground level
and all that (I) sky
Always cutting out

Wading in water
rigor of cold

They do not know what a syllable is

The protection of sleep
The protection of sheep

Patron of stealthy action
The stealthy

Real and personal property

Paper money and tender acts

Fiction of administrative law
Fathers dare not name me

Chasm dogma scoops out

The invention of law
the codification of money

Democracy and property
Rules are guards and fences

In the court of black earth
to be infinite

———

Consumable commodity

a Zero-sum game
and consequent

spiral haze stricture

Distance or outness

Phrase edged away

Money runs after goods
Men desire money

Wages of labor
Wages in a mother country

Authorial withdrawal

Will as fourth wall

My heavy heavy child

hatchet-heartedness
of the Adversary

On anonimity Anonimity

———

in mum
in arm
in ale

s
a in tone
open
v
i e s
company
n
o
fluent
p

Wedged destiny shed [cancel whole] halter measure mutiny Act Wars   Child
regical

Mute
fluke
squall

Human |authoritative| human!
Record They cumbered the ground.
Freak inside the heart
Secret fact a title given
THE REVISER

About the Author

SUSAN HOWE, the author of thirteen books of poetry, has been an actress and assistant stage designer at the Gate Theatre in Dublin, a painter, radio producer, and literary critic. The daughter of a Harvard Law School professor and an Irish playwright and actress, she graduated from the Boston Museum School of Fine Arts in 1961 and received first prize in painting. During the next ten years her work evolved from painting to drawing with words to writing poetry exclusively in 1971. She has been inspired by Charles Olson, painter Agnes Martin, and historian Richard Slotkin, as well as by Emily Dickinson and early Puritan writers, including Cotton Mather.

In 1985 she was one of ten American poets at the New Poetics Colloquium in Vancouver, British Columbia, where she returned in 1987 as visiting foreign artist-in-residence. During the summer of 1988 she was one of five American poets at the Rencontres Internationales de Poésie Contemporaine in Tarascon, France.

She is Professor of English at the State University of New York–Buffalo. She has received the Before Columbus Foundation American Book Award twice, in 1980 for *Secret History of the Dividing Line,* and in 1987 for her critical study, *My Emily Dickinson.* She has also received the first Roy Harvey Pearce Award for a Poet and Critic for her book *The Birth-mark* (Wesleyan, 1993).

Her most recent works are *Frame Structures: Early Poems, 1974–1979* (1995), and her essay "Sorting Facts; or Nineteen Ways of Looking at Marker," in *Beyond Document: Essays on Nonfiction Film* (Wesleyan, 1996), edited by Charles Warren.

Howe lives in Guilford, Connecticut, when she is not teaching in Buffalo.